Joanie Boney Books

multicultural and multiracial

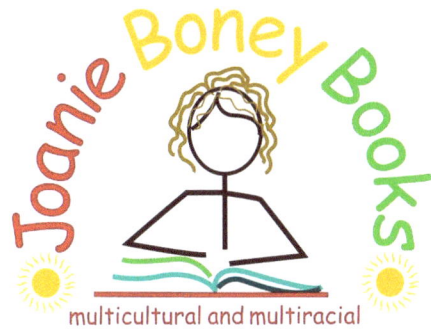

www.joanieboneybooks.com

Thank you for purchasing a Joanie Boney book!

Printed in the USA

About the Author: Joanie Boney Books are multicultural and multiracial reflecting the true America.

Illustrator: Natasha Kostovska

U-Impact Publishing LLC

I would like to know how much you liked my book so please leave a review.

Learning with Lillie

COUNTING FROM 1-20

Written by: Joanie Boney

Illustrations: Natasha Kostovska

1,2,3,4,5 isn't that fun?

...6, 7, 8, 9, 10 counting is fun!

... 11, 12, 13, 14, 15

learning fast you see.

Now let's try it again.
Count what you see
and tell me.

1

One red apple
good to eat.

2

Two yellow pears
nice and sweet.

3

Three blueberries
all in a bunch.

4

Four oranges
sweet and plump.

5

Five green grapes
I will eat them up!

6

Six little lemons
that's enough.

7

Seven red tomatoes
did you know
that's
a fruit?

8

Eight blue plums,
let's make some juice.

9

Nine lemon limes
all green and tart.

10

Ten strawberries
they look like hearts.

11

Eleven bananas
my favorite fruit.

12

Twelve water melons juicy and sweet.

13

Thirteen cherries
dark and red.

14

Fourteen elderberries enough said.

15

Fifteen honey dews
yellow like the sun.

16

Sixteen kiwis they are a lot of fun.

17

Seventeen mangos
I eat all day.

18

Eighteen peaches, pie is on the way.

19

Nineteen pineapples
delicious you see.

Now that you have
learned to count
to twenty go color*the story
and make it real sunny.